PAINT POURING

Project Book

Learn how to create a collection of paint pouring projects!

5 projects inside

INTRODUCTION

Welcome to the wonderful world of Paint Pouring!

This kit has been specifically designed for adults only.

Learning a new skill is always exciting – we're here to help you get started. Paint pouring is a quick and super easy way of creating a beautiful piece of fluid abstract art. You can pick as many colours as you like, a little bit of pouring medium to thin your paint, some cups to pour from and away you go!

Anyone can learn to pour paint, and the great thing about it is – there's no wrong or right way to do it. You can be as creative as you like, even as a beginner. Every piece of work will be unique and different in its own way. If you are a little nervous to start pouring paint, (as it can get very messy, very quickly) start with just one or two colours. You can add an additional colour for each further make you try. Even with only a few options, you can mix your colours to create lighter or darker shades to use as extra additions.

You can even re-use your materials, which is even better. Not only can you use your pouring cup as a drying rack, (we'll get more into this later) you can also re-use your excess paint to create new masterpieces! Why not add some extra detail to your piece? Try placing some gold leaf or dried flowers onto your canvas for an eye-catching look. Or, see how creative you can get by moving your paint in different ways with items found around your home - string, a toothpick, or even a straw to blow on your paint.

This kit provides everything you need to make your first piece of art, which means getting started is easy. We have included four other projects within this book to help you along the way. Just like any new craft, paint pouring can be a little tricky at first. Experiment with different colours and techniques. But most importantly, enjoy yourself.

Let's get started on your paint pouring journey.

KIT CONTENTS

WHAT'S INCLUDED:

· 4x Smooth pebbles
· Marbling ink (2 colours x 5ml)
· 1x Wooden stirrer
· 2x Paper cups
· 1 Pair disposable gloves

WHAT YOU'LL NEED:

· Toothpick/skewers/plastic spoons
· Silicone Oil (optional)
· Small canvas boards (for further designs)
· Lots of cups to mix your colours & medium together
· A small paintbrush
· A drying rack or something strong to prop your work up against to dry
· Pouring medium (optional) or water

Ingredients:
Acrylic resin emulsion, Blue (Phtalogyanie) water. White (Titanium dioxide),
Propane diol-1,3, Propylparaben, Texanol.

THE BASICS:

Paint pouring is all about creating a unique piece of abstract art. After mixing your chosen paint colours or marbling inks with water, distilled water or acrylic medium, you can then pour your paint onto your chosen surface, creating a beautiful piece of fluid art.

When starting your paint pouring journey, you will need to mix each of your acrylic colours individually with a little bit of pouring medium. This will improve the fluidity of your paint, making it much easier to pour. How much medium to use all depends on the thickness of the paint you have chosen. As a general rule for acrylic paint - we use 1 part paint to 2 part acrylic medium. If your paint is still a little bit thick after adding your medium, you can add a tiny bit of distilled water to loosen up the consistency even further.

Acrylic paint is water based, and one of the most versatile paints to use for paint pouring. It's a great paint to use on your paint pouring journey. What's more, it can also be thinned out easily to allow your paint to flow effortlessly. Do be careful, however, when you are paint pouring. Acrylic paints have a tendency to dry quickly. If you want your colours to romantically blend into one another, you may have to give your piece of work that extra helping hand - tilting it will achieve the end result you want before it dries!

Once you have mastered the technique of paint pouring, (which you will pick up in no time) you will start to feel more confident in adding additional colours to your work. This will help when you are ready to add additional steps! A beautiful technique to enhance your paint pour, is to add a few drops of silicone oil to your paints. The silicone oil works by rising to the surface, bringing your paint colours with it. This technique creates a beautiful cell like movement in the paint – you will see this as we move through the process!

Top Tips - Before starting any craft involving paint, (and there will be lots of paint) always cover your work surface with an old sheet, plastic bags or old newspaper will do the trick!
Pop your disposable gloves on before you start mixing any paint together as things are about to get very messy!

There are so many different ways to paint pour, but we have chosen our favourite four to show you!

Dirty Pour

The dirty pour technique is created by layering your individual paints all in one cup, (it's good to do this in a repetitive sequence so your colours alternate in your cup) and then simply pouring it onto your surface. This is one of the most versatile ways of paint pouring. Lots of additional techniques can then be created and follow on a dirty pour.

Puddle Pour

A puddle pour is one step on from the dirty pour. To do this, you go through the process of creating your dirty pour cup. This time, instead of pouring the contents of your cup onto the surface in one go, you will gently create separate 'puddles' of paint. You can then decide which way the paint moves by tilting your work surface in lots of different directions.

Basic/Clean Pour

A clean pour (some call this a basic pour) is probably the most simple of pours and a great one for beginners. This is created by pouring the colours you have chosen one at a time onto your surface. This can be done so they don't touch each other, or this can be done so you layer them on top of each other which will create a little bit more of a complex pattern. You can also expand this technique by adding a few drops of silicone to your paint at the very beginning to achieve 'cells' within your paint (more on this later).

Flip Cup

A flip cup pour is exactly what it says on the tin! This technique is probably the most messy but the most fun! This is achieved by filling your cup full of paint, laying your surface on top of the cup and quickly flipping everything over! By flipping your cup in this way, you will create beautiful blends of colours as well as unique contemporary patterns. Once you have tried this method, why not try adding some extra design onto your painting - maybe some dried flowers pressed on top? Or gently layer some gold leaf? (We will get onto this later!)

Top Tips - Once your paint resembles the consistency of a warmed syrup, you are onto a winner! This should pour easily, but watch out for any visible lumps - this may mean the paint is still too thick. If this is the case, add a tiny bit more of your medium but be careful - you don't want it too watery either!

SO EXTRA!

Once you have created your paint pouring masterpieces, there are many ways you can add that little extra something to them! At the beginning of the booklet, we spoke about adding gold leaf to obtain an eye-catching look. Or how about running a toothpick through your paint before it dries and creating some feathering? You could even use a straw to blow air over your paint and manipulate the way it moves in different directions.
Below are a few ideas for you to try.

Puddle Pour with air

Once you're happy with your covered surface, you can use air (blow through a straw) to create texture with your paint whilst it's still wet.

Flip Cup with gold leaf

Once your flip cup canvas is complete - but before it dries - use a small paintbrush or a wooden stick and gently pick up your individual flakes of gold leaf. VERY gently, place these on your canvas being careful not to move your paint in any way!

Using up excess paint

After all of your paint pours, you will find you are left with a little bit of blended paint in the bottom of each cup. Don't let this go to waste! Use the remainder of the paint in the bottom of your cups to pour over another surface.

WARNINGS!

All the makes included in this book are designed specifically for adults.

Keep all ingredients and finished products out of the reach of children.

Some ingredients may irritate; always avoid contact with skin and eyes. If ingredients come into contact with eyes or skin, wash with cold water immediately.

Do not ingest; if accidentally ingested drink water and seek medical advice.

We recommend wearing old clothes or overalls when partaking in creative activities. Cover work surfaces to avoid mess.

MAKE
WITH KIT
CONTENTS

PEBBLE POURING

PEBBLE POURING

With this make, we will show you how to create these cute pebble designs using the 'dirty pour' method!

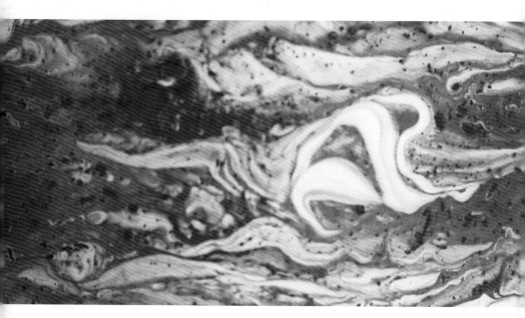

KIT INCLUDES
·4x Smooth pebbles
·Marbling ink (2 colours x 5ml)
·1x Wooden stirrer
·2x Paper cups
·1 Pair of disposable gloves

METHOD

1. Making sure your work surface is covered, collect your pebbles, two inks, cups, wooden stirrer & gloves.

2. Next, pour your colours into individual cups and mix. Make sure there are no bubbles or lumps of ink present. If you think your ink is too thick you can add a tiny bit of water (preferably distilled) or pouring medium.

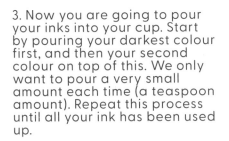

3. Now you are going to pour your inks into your cup. Start by pouring your darkest colour first, and then your second colour on top of this. We only want to pour a very small amount each time (a teaspoon amount). Repeat this process until all your ink has been used up.

4. Now it's time for the fun part! Lay your pebbles down on your surface and pour your ink over the top. Do make sure to move your cup as you are pouring to cover the whole surface of your pebble.

5. At this stage, you will start to see your inks flowing effortlessly over your pebbles. Your two colours will create a beautiful pattern.

6. Once you are happy and both of your pebbles have been covered, gently lift them one by one and elevate them to dry. You can do this by placing them on top of an object where the excess paint can run off. For this example, we chose to turn the cup we were using upside down and rest the pebble on top. Leave to dry for 24-48hrs.

NOTES

Use the space below to make your own personal notes on the previous project to help when you come back to make it again!

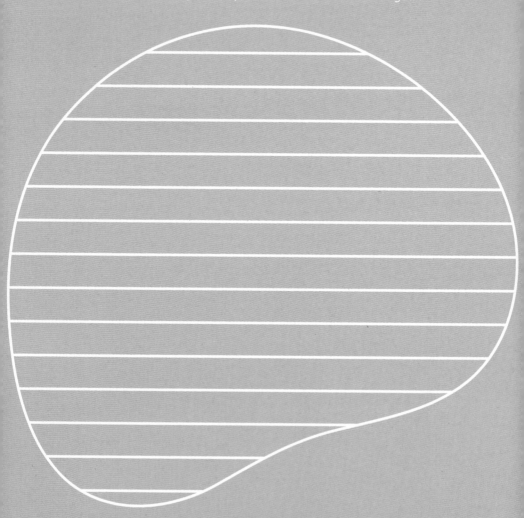

ABSTRACT
CANVAS

ABSTRACT CANVAS

Experience the puddle pouring technique! This design will take you through another fun and easy way to paint pour.

YOU WILL NEED
·Paint (4/5 colours)
·Cups
·Canvas
·Gloves

METHOD

1. Start by getting your canvas ready, along with the colours that you want to pour. For puddle pouring, we would recommend choosing 4-5 colours. Place them in separate cups. Make sure to mix in your acrylic medium as before. You will then need an extra empty cup that you will use for Step 2.

2. Now you have your colours ready, start by pouring a little bit of each colour into the empty cup. Alternate between each colour until you have used them all up and your paint is now layered in one cup.

3. Start to pour your paint slowly onto your canvas. Do this until the paint is the size of a 50p piece. As you lift your cup up, slightly roll it to prevent any dripping. Then move to another area of your canvas and pour again – thus creating 'puddles' of paint.

4. Once you are happy with your puddles, slowly start to tilt your canvas. Move it around until you have rotated a full circle.

5. If the paint hasn't reached the edges, you may find you need to add a little extra paint. You can use the excess paint that has gathered in the bottom of your cup.

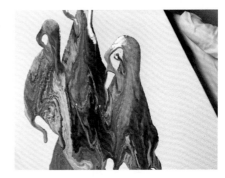

6. Continue tilting. This time, raise your canvas slightly higher to encourage the paint to travel across the canvas. When you are happy, lay it flat and leave to dry for 24-48 hours.

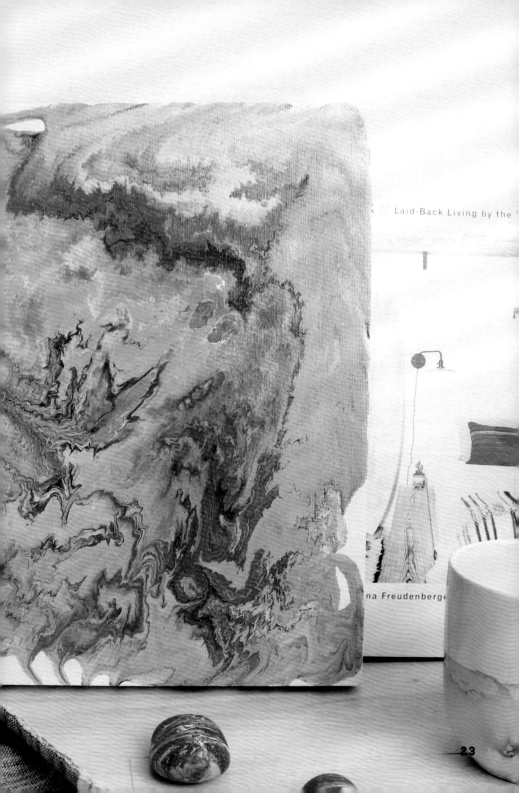

NOTES

Use the space below to make your own personal notes on the previous project to help when you come back to make it again!

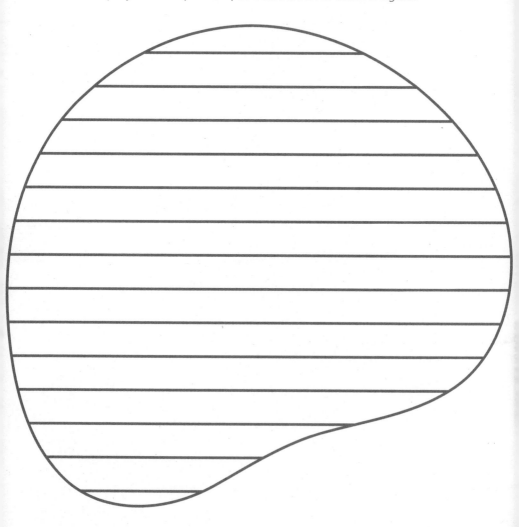

COASTER

COASTER

Following on from your pebble paint pouring, we are now going to show you a way you can re-use all that excess paint. Remember when we said paint pouring can get a bit messy? Well here it is!

YOU WILL NEED
·Coaster
·Paint (approx. 4colours)
·Gloves
·Cups

METHOD

1. You still have more paint left on your surface. By now, you may also be feeling more confident in your paint pouring abilities. If this is the case, add another colour into the mix. Gently pour it on top of the excess paint you already have left.

2. As we have used different shades of blue for this one, we're going to add some white to the mix. White is great to add to any colour combo, because it will enhance and lighten your design. Add a couple of drops on top.

3. Holding your coaster firmly in one hand, gently lower onto the paint. Make sure the whole coaster is going to be covered.

4. Using two fingers, very gently, but firmly, hold the coaster in place for 30 seconds.
Be extremely careful not to move it in any way!

5. Holding onto the corners tightly, and being careful not to smudge the paint with your fingers, gently lift your coaster up. You may notice that there are areas of your coaster that haven't been covered by the paint. If this is the case – lay it back down and repeat step 4.

6. Gently lift your coaster up to reveal your paint pour design. You will notice that your paint will still be moving and dripping to form its final pattern. Once you are happy with your coaster, lay it down flat on a paper plate so it is slightly elevated from the table and will be easy to move once dry. Leave to dry for 24-48hrs.

NOTES

Use the space below to make your own personal notes on the previous project to help when you come back to make it again!

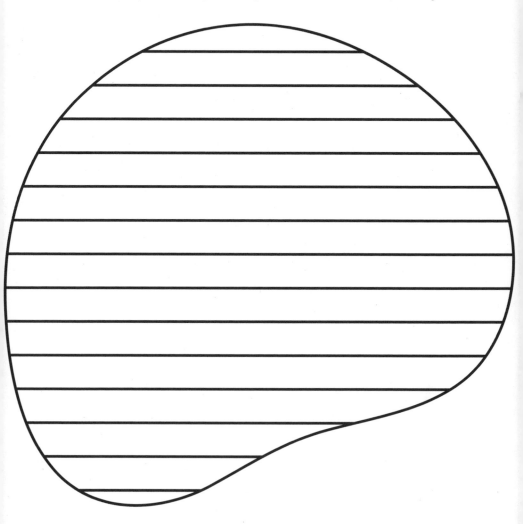

SILICONE
CANVAS

SILICONE CANVAS

With this design we will explain the 'basic clean pour' method using silicone.

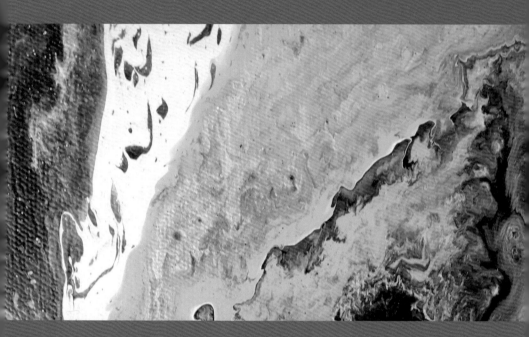

YOU WILL NEED
- Paint (approx 4 colours)
- Cups
- Canvas
- Gloves
- Frame (optional)
- Silicone oil

METHOD

1. Start by choosing your 4 colours and popping them into separate cups - once again mixing each one with marble medium. This time, add a few drops of silicone oil (2-3 drops) to each cup. Silicone oil will create a beautiful cell affect with your paint.

2. Laying your canvas board flat, start by pouring your first colour (we've used our lightest one to start) and pour until you reach the size of a 10p piece. Then, take your second colour and pour on top of this.

3. Repeat this process with colours 3 and 4. Once you have done this, start your second puddle following the same sequence.

4. Do this until you have 3 or 4 separate puddles of paint on your canvas. You will notice that your puddles will start to blend together.

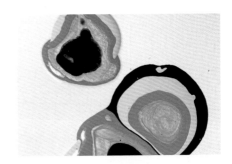

5. To encourage your paint to move more freely, gently lift your canvas up and start to tilt it around. Move it until you have completed a full circle and your paint has reached all corners of your canvas.

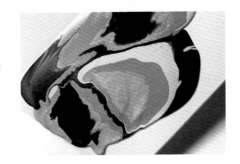

6. Leave to dry flat for 24-48 hours.

NOTES

Use the space below to make your own personal notes on the previous project to help when you come back to make it again!

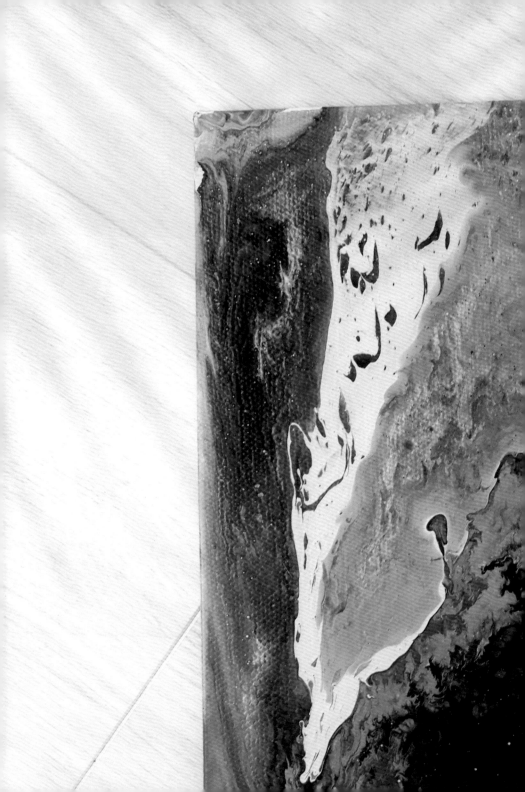

FLIP CUP
CANVAS

FLIP CUP CANVAS

This next design focuses on the 'flip cup' method. So cups at the ready! Let's begin.

YOU WILL NEED

- Paint (approx. 4colours)
- Gloves
- Cups
- Canvas
- Gold leaf (optional)
- Frame (optional)

METHOD

1. Start by getting your canvas ready, and choosing your colours. For this method, we recommend using 3-4 colours, popping each colour into a separate cup. In each cup, mix 1 part paint to 2 part medium as before. You will then need an extra cup that you will use for Step 2.

2. Now you have your colours ready, start pouring a little bit of each colour into the empty cup. Alternate between each colour until you have used up your colours and all your paint is in the one cup.

3. Place your canvas (canvas side down) on top of your cup so that your cup is balancing in the center of your canvas. Holding the base of the cup with one hand, and the top of your canvas with the other hand - Flip!

4. Very gently, release your cup and let your cup of paint flow. You will notice the colours from your cup instantly blending into one another as they roll over the canvas.

5. Once again, very gently tilt your canvas. This time, raise it slightly higher to make your colours mingle into one another covering every piece of your board.

6. Leave to dry flat for 24-48 hours.

7. When dried if you have gold leaf, nows the time to add it!

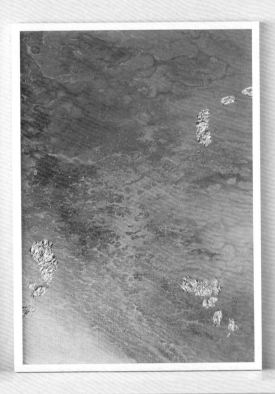

NOTES

Use the space below to make your own personal notes on the previous project to help when you come back to make it again!

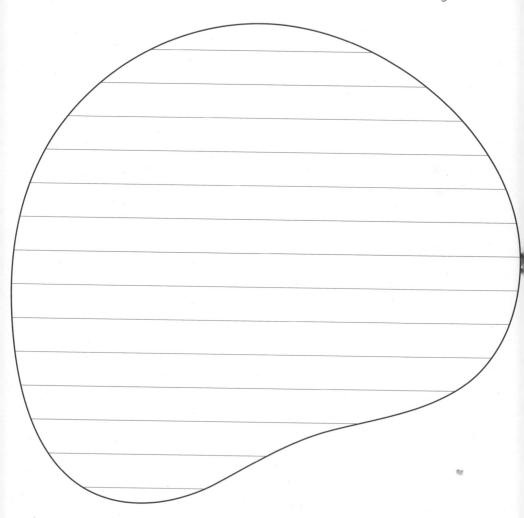